Abdul's Garden Grows

Author & Photographer: Denise Angelle

"Thank you" to Abdul Kareem Solomon for sharing his

passion & expertise in Horticulture.

ISBN 13: 978-0-9809403-8-1
ISBN 10: 098940389
Comfort-Heed Publications
A Division of WORLDSTRENGTH

Abdul's Garden Grows

This Book Belongs To:

NAME: ....

NOTES: ....

....

....

This is Abdul. He has a large vegetable farm in the Greater Accra Region of Ghana, Africa. Abdul studied Horticulture in University and is an expert on growing vegetables. This is the profession that Abdul has chosen for his life. Abdul loves to tend his gardens on the farm!

Some of the beautiful and nutritious vegetables that are grown in the gardens on the farm are lettuce, cabbage, tomatoes, green peppers, cucumbers and onions. These vegetables are all very delicious to eat.

It takes a lot of special care to grow vegetables. First the soil has to be prepared properly and any live weeds must be removed from the soil.

A hoe is a tool used to cultivate the soil so that it is fresh and ready for the planting of new vegetables. If there is any disease or bacteria in the soil it must be treated with special agricultural chemicals.

A shovel is used to dig a valley around all garden beds. This allows water to gather in the valleys which provides continued moisture for the soil. The sources of water for Abdul's gardens

are rain, hand-watering from the pond and a sprinkler system. Some dried mulch on top of the soil also helps retain the moisture and provides protection as the plants first start to grow.

Some of the cultural practises involved in growing vegetables in Abdul's gardens are preparation of the field, nursing, transplanting, watering, weeding, agricultural chemical spraying and the application of fertilizer when necessary.

Most vegetables are nursed before being transplanted into large garden beds. Some other vegetables such as cucumbers, squash and green beans are sown directly on the field with seeds.

The nursery bed, where most of Abdul's vegetables start growing, is a small sized bed of soil where the seeds first germinate. The two main types of nursing are broadcasting and the drill method. Broadcasting is the spreading of seeds over the soil and the drill method is done using a stick to create a shallow line in the soil to place the seeds in and then lightly covering the seeds with soil. The nursery bed is first treated with a chemical to control some harmful soil pathogens such as nematodes, which cause root-knot disease and drains the plant's nutrients destroying it or causing a low yield. After nursing, the bed is covered with dried grass to protect the seeds from the direct impact of the sun and to allow the soil to stay moist. This helps the seeds to germinate well. The dried grass, or mulch, is taken off after two days to prevent the seedlings from growing tall; instead they will grow broad and strong. The seedlings are allowed to grow for about two to three weeks depending on how rich the nursery bed soil is. The richer the soil is with nutrients, the faster the plants grow.

We will now follow the process of growing lettuce at Abdul's farm. Lettuce starts to grow in the nursery before it grows in the large garden bed. The seeds are broadcasted generously on top of the nursery garden bed. A light covering of soil is then sprinkled over the seeds. It is important that the seeds are close to the surface and not too deep in the soil or they will not be able to survive. The light covering of soil allows the seeds to take root. Dried grass is then placed on top for temporary protection. The nursery lettuce grows very close together which helps the tiny plants to start developing.

At a special time of partial maturity (approximately 2 months) the small lettuce plants must be removed from the nursery and transplanted in the prepared garden bed where they will continue to grow until full maturity. The transplanting is a very delicate and gentle process. All the precious roots growing on the lettuce seedlings must be removed carefully from the nursery bed soil.

The lettuce seedlings are carried to the garden bed for transplanting. A small hole is created for the roots to be submerged and then they are enclosed under the soil with a gentle squeeze of the fingers.

The lettuce seedlings are planted in even rows throughout the garden bed. Strings with posts are used as guidelines to help keep the planting straight. In this particular bed, 7 seedlings were planted across the width and 112 were planted along the length in each row. The planting for this garden bed totaled 784 lettuce seedlings.

After planting, water is then collected from the local water source and the garden bed is carefully hand-watered to continue the growth process of the lettuce. Some of the important factors determining the success of the lettuce plants are sun, water, disease and predators.

If there is just the right amount of sun and water, with no disease, insects or animals to destroy the plants, most or all will flourish to produce the desired harvest of beautiful heads of lettuce.

The lettuce beds are clean and orderly and have the natural elements to face, such as the sun and rain. The sprinkler irrigation system is installed as a back-up for water when needed. This draws water from the local dam and operates with a water pump machine.

The workers on the farm watch over the crops carefully. They also continue to hand-water the gardens when necessary and keep the weeds out of the beds. There is a lot of tender care and trust in God that goes into the production of these wonderful vegetables.

With Abdul's dedication and effort invested and all other satisfactory elements in place, the lettuce grows faithfully and produces a beautiful finished product. After the lettuce is harvested it is sold to street market vendors, restaurants, supermarkets and individuals. Many people are buying large quantities of lettuce and other vegetables as they realize the health benefits of eating nutritious food and also the great taste vegetables add to meals. This lettuce harvest proved to be very successful and profitable for Abdul!

Abdul's Garden Grows

GLOSSARY

Agriculture: The science or practice of farming which can include cultivating soil, production of crops and/or animal rearing.

Bacteria: Also called germs, bacteria are microscopic organisms, not visible to the eye, that are dangerous when they cause infection.

Broadcasting: The method of sprinkling seeds by hand on the soil.

Chemicals: Substances used to control or stop crop-harming organisms or disease.

Cultivate: To prepare and use land by breaking up and loosening the soil for planting crops and/or gardening.

Disease: An illness or abnormal condition caused by infection.

Germinate: When a plant begins to grow or develop.

Horticulture: The science or practice of garden cultivation and management.

Maturity: The state of being in full growth or development.

Nematodes: Microscopic worms, many of them parasites of insects, plants or animals. A handful of soil can contain thousands of them.

Nursery: A special garden bed where young plants are first grown closely together before transplanting into a larger garden.

Nutritious: Describes food that is beneficial for people's health due to nutrients contained inside (vitamins, minerals, antioxidants, etc.).

Pathogens: Bacteria, virus or other microorganisms that can cause illness and disease.

Predators: Creatures that can harm the plants development or life.

Seedlings: A young plant grown from seed and not from a cutting.

Transplanting: To move or transfer plants to another location.

ACTIVITIES

1. What profession did Abdul choose? ....

2. Where did Abdul learn his profession? ....

3. What does a Horticulturalist do? ....

4. Name and draw 4 green vegetables that can grow in a garden:
....

5. Name 3 vegetables that can grow from directly planting seeds without a nursery: ....

6. Give an example of a vegetable that starts to grow in a nursery:

....

7. What are 2 natural elements that plants face in the garden?

....

8. What are the duties that the workers on the farm must fulfill to care for the plants in the gardens? ....

....

9. Name 4 people or places that Abdul sells his lettuce to:

....

10. What do you think the benefits would be of growing your own vegetables in a garden? ....

....

11. What vegetables do you like to eat and name 4 different meals that can be made with vegetables cooked in them?

....

....

....

12. After doing your own research, name some ways that eating nutritious food benefits people's health? ....

....

....

....

13. If you had to choose a profession at this time, what would it be and why would you choose it? ....

....

....

14. Draw a picture of yourself at work in your chosen profession: